MEASURING A COMPANY'S
FOREIGN TAX CREDIT POSITION

by

Henry Louie and Gerald Silverstein
Office of Tax Analysis, U.S. Department of Treasury
and
Donald J. Rousslang
Hawaii State Department of Taxation

OTA Paper 97   **October 2006**

OTA Papers is an occasional series of reports on the research, models, and data sets developed to inform and improve Treasury's tax policy analysis. The papers are works in progress and subject to revision. Views and opinions expressed are those of the authors and do not necessarily represent official Treasury positions or policy. OTA Papers are distributed in order to document OTA analytic methods and data and invite discussion and suggestions for revision and improvement. Comments are welcome and should be directed to the authors.

Office of Tax Analysis
Department of the Treasury
Washington, DC 20220

The authors thank Charles Boynton, Harry Grubert, Don Kiefer and William Randolph for helpful comments and discussion. The views expressed in this paper are those of the authors and do not necessarily reflect the views of the Treasury Department.

Abstract

A number of authors have tried to discover how the residual U.S. tax on foreign corporate earnings (the U.S. tax after the foreign tax credit) affects business decisions. Some of them inferred the residual tax from data in the company's financial statement, whereas others used the residual tax reported in the company's income tax return. In the present study, we point out problems with both approaches. For instance, we show that in many cases, the two approaches yield different results for the same firm. We then compare the generally accepted measures of the residual tax with a third measure that, at least conceptually, should reliably reveal whether the company anticipates owing a residual tax for the year, after accounting for its ability to carry unused foreign tax credits over to prior or future years. We find that this third measure does not accord well with the commonly used measures of the company's foreign tax credit position. We believe that our results, therefore, draw into question the conclusions of the earlier studies that tried to capture the incentives imparted by the residual U.S. tax.

Table of Contents

Table of Figures

Introduction

A number of authors have tried to discover how the residual U.S. tax on foreign earnings of U.S. corporations – the U.S. tax after the credit for foreign income taxes – influences business decisions (Mutti, 1981; Hines and Hubbard, 1990; Altshuler and Newlon, 1993; Altshuler, Newlon and Randolph, 1995; Froot and Hines, 1995; Hines, 1996; Collins, Kemsley and Lang, 1998; and Kemsley, 1998, among others).[1] Some of them relied on information reported in financial statements to infer the residual tax, while others looked at the actual corporate income tax returns.[2] All of them used a dummy variable to represent the foreign tax credit position (i.e., whether or not the company owed a residual tax). In the present paper we show how the residual taxes that are inferred from the financial statements differ from those taken from the tax returns. We also show that the dummy variables used in the earlier studies differ systematically from a variable that should, logically, best represent the incentives imparted by the residual tax. To make clear the limitations of the study from the outset, we do not try to determine the biases that might be present in the earlier studies.

The obvious problem with using data from financial statements to infer the

---

[1] Mutti (1981), Hines and Hubbard (1990), Altshuler and Newlon (1993), and Altshuler, Newlon and Randolph (1995) sought to explain dividend repatriation behavior. Froot and Hines (1995) estimated the effect of U.S. interest allocation rules on borrowing and new investment of U.S. companies. Hines (1996) estimated how after-tax foreign earnings affect the company's dividend payout rate. Collins, Kemsley and Lang (1998) sought to explain how U.S. companies respond to tax incentives to shift income between affiliates in different countries. Kemsley (1998) sought to explain how the U.S. sales source rules affect a company's decision whether to locate new production in the United States or abroad. All of the studies used a variable for the residual U.S. tax in their regressions.

2 Mutti (1981), Hines and Hubbard (1990), Altshuler and Newlon (1993), and Altshuler, Newlon and Randolph (1995) used tax return data, whereas Froot and Hines (1995), Hines (1996), Collins, Kemsley and Lang (1998), and Kemsley (1998) used data from financial statements.

residual tax is that the foreign income and taxes on the financial statement are not the same, even conceptually, as the foreign income and taxes that determine the company's residual U.S. tax. But even the foreign tax credit position actually reported on the tax return may be a poor guide to the incentives being imparted by the residual tax. This is true, because excess foreign tax credits can be carried forward or back to other years.[3] To the extent that the residual tax influences business decisions, it is the final foreign tax credit position for the year that matters, not the current-year position. But this final position is not known until carry-overs are exhausted.[4]

If one is trying to discover the effect of the residual tax on a business decision such as a repatriation of income from a foreign subsidiary, the best variable to use is one that reflects the final position as it is anticipated by the company when the decision is made. In this paper, we devise a variable that logically should reveal the final foreign tax credit position the company anticipates having for the year. The variable is gleaned from the company's tax planning behavior; namely, how the company chooses between two tax provisions for U.S. export profits, the sales source rules (sections 863(b) and 862(a)(6) of the Internal Revenue Code) and Foreign Sales Corporations (FSCs). Of course, this variable is available only for companies that export goods from the United States and only for those few years that data on FSC operations are available,[5] so it is not

---

[3] The American Jobs Creation Act of 2004 changed the rules for credit carryovers. Under the new rules, excess foreign tax credits can be carried back one year and carried forward for ten years. Our data predate the new rules. During the period of our analysis, excess foreign tax credits could be carried forward for only five years or back for two years.

[4] As will be explained later, the final position for the year may not be known, even well after the period in which excess foreign tax credits from the year can be carried forward.

[5] Data on FSC operations are available for the fiscal years 1985 through 1987, 1992, 1996, and 2000. The

always a viable alternative for researchers studying the effects of the residual tax. Nevertheless, it is a useful tool to assess the other variables as measures of the company's foreign tax credit position.

This paper is organized as follows: the next section summarizes briefly the U.S. rules for taxing foreign earnings of U.S. companies. The third section describes the financial statement data on foreign earnings and foreign taxes and shows how they differ from foreign income and creditable foreign taxes that the company reports on its tax return. The fourth section describes our method for inferring the company's final anticipated position. The fifth section describes the data and presents our results. The last section contains a summary and conclusions.

The U.S. Rules for Taxing Foreign Earnings

The United States taxes the worldwide income of U.S. multinational companies, but allows them to defer the tax on earnings of their foreign subsidiaries until the earnings are repatriated. Income from a company's foreign operations that is subject to U.S. tax in the current year is called foreign-source income (FSI) and is reported on Form 1118 (Foreign Tax Credit – Corporations) of the U.S. parent's tax return. FSI consists mainly of the following items: dividends received from foreign subsidiaries, measured gross of foreign withholding taxes; foreign income taxes deemed paid on the earnings

---

FSC program has been eliminated, so no new data on its operations are forthcoming. The corporate income tax return (Form 1120) contained an entry for dividends from a FSC or former FSC, but the FSC income did not always show up as dividends to the parent company in the year it was earned. The corporate form filed to claim a foreign tax credit (Form 1118) has a category for income from a FSC or prior FSC, but the basket contains only a special kind of FSC income.

that underlie these dividends, or the "gross-up" for foreign income taxes;[6] foreign-source interest income; rents and royalties received for exports of technology and other services; income earned by foreign branches; and profits from U.S. goods exports that are treated as foreign source income under the sales source rules (described in more detail below). The U.S. parent must also pay current U.S. tax on certain income of controlled foreign corporations (CFCs)[7] under subpart F of the Internal Revenue Code, whether or not the income is actually repatriated. For the most part, subpart F prevents companies from deferring the U.S. tax on income from investments that are highly mobile and therefore easy to locate in low-tax jurisdictions, such as investments in financial assets and international shipping. Finally, taxpayers must deduct certain domestic expenses from FSI including some of their domestic interest expenses, some of their domestic research and development expenses, and some of their home-office overhead expenses.

As part of its system of worldwide taxation, the United States allows a credit for foreign taxes, which can be subtracted from the latent U.S. tax. The foreign tax credit equals the foreign income taxes paid on the foreign earnings underlying the FSI plus foreign withholding taxes, or the U.S. tax rate times the FSI, whichever is less. FSI is assigned to a "basket," based on the type of income. The U.S. tax liability and foreign tax

---

6 When the U.S. parent owns 10 percent or more of the stock of a foreign subsidiary, it grosses up the dividends it receives from the subsidiary to get the underlying foreign earnings before foreign income taxes. The foreign earnings are defined according to U.S. tax principles and may bear little resemblance to the taxable income as defined by the host country. The foreign earnings generally are close to the standard accounting definition of income ("book" income), especially when the foreign activity is manufacturing.

7 A CFC is a foreign corporation in which U.S. shareholders, each of whom owns 10 percent or more of the corporation's stock, collectively own more than 50 percent of the corporation's stock.

credit are calculated separately for each basket. The baskets have been modified by recent legislation,[8] but for the period covered by our data, the main baskets were for passive income (portfolio dividends, interest, rents and royalties from unrelated parties abroad or from non-controlled foreign corporations), financial services income, international shipping income, and general limitation income (income from a foreign affiliate in an active trade or business that is not included in one of the other baskets). Other baskets were for dividends from so-called "section 902" corporations (foreign subsidiaries in which the U.S. parent owns between 10 percent and 50 percent of the equity), for income from foreign subsidiaries engaged in international shipping, for interest income on which foreign withholding tax has been paid at a rate of 5 percent or more, for dividends from a FSC or former FSC, for income from foreign trading companies, and for dividends from a Domestic International Sales Corporation (DISC) or former DISC.[9] There was a separate basket for each section 902 corporation, but all of the company's FSI from majority-owned foreign subsidiaries, and the attendant foreign taxes, were lumped together within each of the other baskets.

If the interest, rents or royalties were received from a CFC, the U.S. parent was allowed to "look through" to the activity that generates the income, so these payments were put into the same basket as the dividends the parent received from the CFC. For example, if the U.S. parent financed a CFC's operations partly with an equity investment and partly with a loan, and if the CFC earned income only from manufacturing activities,

---

[8]   The American Jobs Creation Act of 2004 reduced the number of baskets from nine to two. Under the new law, all FSI, except for passive income which retains its own basket, is placed into the general basket.

9   The DISC, a special tax provision for U.S. export profits, was replaced by the FSC program in 1985.

then both the dividends and the interest that the parent receives from the CFC went into the basket for general limitation income (the "general" basket). The general basket accounts for the lion's share of the FSI earned by U.S. manufacturing companies; for example, in 1992 and 1996 (the sample years for the quantitative analysis that follows), this basket contained on average 94 percent of the FSI of these companies. Under the old rules, it was possible for a company to have many foreign tax credit baskets, and to have a different credit position in each basket. For example, a U.S. parent with foreign subsidiaries in manufacturing and financial services could have had excess foreign tax credits in the general basket and at the same time owe a residual U.S. tax on FSI in the financial services basket.

Since 1987, the U.S. parent has had to pool earnings and income taxes across years for each foreign subsidiary. When dividends are paid from the pool to the U.S. parent, the foreign taxes attached to the dividends are calculated by taking the ratio of the dividends to the pooled earnings and multiplying it times the foreign income taxes in the pool.

Problems Encountered When Inferring the Company's Foreign Tax Credit Position from Its Financial Statement

Differences between FSI and Foreign Income as Reported in the Financial Statement

Foreign income reported in the company's financial statement consists of pre-tax foreign earnings of its majority-owned affiliates with a deduction for minority interest, plus after-tax income from its minority-owned foreign subsidiaries. There are several major differences between foreign income and FSI. One is that interest, rents and royalties from a foreign subsidiary are part of the U.S. parent company's FSI, but they are expenses of the subsidiary so they are not reported as income in the parent's consolidated financial statement. A second major difference is that the sales source rules for U.S. exports allow the U.S. parent to include some of the income from U.S. exports in FSI, whereas little, if any, of this income is included in foreign income in financial statements. A third major difference arises from differences in timing between when foreign income is earned and when it is included in FSI: The financial statement includes all foreign earnings, whether or not they are repatriated to the U.S. parent, whereas FSI includes the earnings of foreign subsidiaries only when they are repatriated by the U.S. parent, or are deemed to have been repatriated under subpart F (although FSI does include income of foreign branches). Also, FSI can include dividends paid from income earned by its foreign subsidiaries in a prior year and retained abroad. A fourth major difference is that FSI excludes losses of foreign subsidiaries, whereas such losses automatically reduce net foreign earnings reported in financial statements. A fifth major difference is that the domestic expenses allocated to FSI are not deducted from foreign income in financial statements.

The above-listed differences are potentially important. For example, in 1992 and 1996 interest, rents and royalties, and gross export income included in FSI under the sales source rules accounted, on average, for 35 percent of gross FSI of all U.S. manufacturing companies. In those years, profitable CFCs of U.S. manufacturing parents averaged more than $71.6 billion per year in earnings after foreign taxes, but the unprofitable CFCs of these same parents averaged annual losses of $12.8 billion and the dividends from the

CFCs averaged only $27.1 billion per year, including deemed dividends under subpart F. Domestic expenses allocated to FSI averaged $43.6 billion, or 36 percent of gross FSI.

There are also a number of other (less important) differences between FSI and foreign income as reported in financial statements. In the period of our data, income from U.S. exports deemed earned by a FSC was included in FSI if the FSC paid a dividend to the U.S. parent, but the FSC income usually did not appear as part of foreign income in financial statements. FSI in the passive income basket includes rents or royalties, or interest on loans that comes from unrelated parties or from minority-owned foreign subsidiaries, but such income is not included in foreign income reported in financial statements. FSI in the section 902 baskets includes the gross-up for foreign corporate income taxes attached to the dividends from minority-owned foreign subsidiaries, but excludes the earnings that were not repatriated, whereas the foreign income reported in financial statements includes the parent's share of all after-tax earnings of the minority-owned foreign subsidiaries.

Another potential source of difference between foreign earnings and FSI may lie in the divergent consolidation rules under Generally Accepted Accounting Principles (GAAP) and U.S. tax rules. In general terms, the GAAP consolidation rules are significantly more inclusive than their tax equivalent. For instance, the consolidated financial group encompasses all of the company's greater-than-50-percent-owned subsidiaries, both domestic and foreign, with a deduction for minority interests. For subsidiaries that are 20-50 percent controlled, a pro-rata share is included under the

11

equity method of accounting. If the company owns less than 20 percent of the subsidiary, only dividends from that subsidiary are included in the consolidated group's income.

This contrasts with the rules for tax consolidation, which allow only those domestic subsidiaries of which the U.S. parent owns at least 80 percent to be consolidated onto the parent's tax return. No deductions are permitted to account for minority interests. These disparities will necessarily create differences between foreign income and FSI for any group other than a U.S. parent and its wholly-owned domestic subsidiary with no foreign operations or holdings, or a U.S. parent with only portfolio holdings in a foreign company[10].

The divergent definitions of the consolidated group result in asymmetrical computations of foreign earnings. First, the tax consolidated group omits all FSI and foreign losses of 50-80-percent owned domestic subsidiaries, whereas these are reflected in the foreign earnings of the financial consolidated group. Second, the U.S. parent is never allowed to use losses in a foreign subsidiary to offset income on its U.S. tax return, whereas the foreign subsidiary losses are included on the consolidated financial statement. It follows that foreign loss-subsidiaries will in all cases drive book FSI down relative to taxable FSI.

Differences between Creditable Foreign Taxes Reported on Tax Returns and Foreign Income Taxes Reported in Financial Statements

Foreign income taxes associated with foreign earnings retained abroad are not reported on the company's U.S. tax return, but they are part of foreign taxes included in

---

[10] In the second hypothetical structure, both the tax- and book-consolidated groups would include only dividends (without a gross-up) and no losses from the foreign company.

its financial statement. However, the foreign income taxes reported on the tax return may differ from those in the financial statement, even if the company repatriates exactly the same amount as its foreign earnings for the year. One reason is that the foreign income taxes that accompany dividends from a subsidiary on the tax return are calculated using the average rate of foreign tax on the subsidiary's pool of post-1986 earnings from which the dividends were drawn, so the associated creditable taxes may not be the same as the foreign income tax paid in the current year. Another reason is that income taxes paid by minority-owned foreign subsidiaries are not included in the foreign taxes in financial statements, but the creditable foreign taxes associated with dividends in the 902 baskets are included on tax returns. Finally, there may be discrepancies between the definition of income taxes used for the financial statements and creditable foreign taxes (defined in section 901 of the IRC).

Other Problems in Inferring Foreign Tax Credit Positions from Financial Statement Data

An important problem in determining foreign tax credit positions from financial statements is that the financial statements do not break down the foreign income and foreign taxes according to the separate limitation baskets. The lack of basket detail in the financial statements reduces their usefulness for inferring foreign tax credit positions. For example, although the bulk of FSI for U.S. parent companies in manufacturing goes into the general basket, some of these companies have sizable FSI in the financial services basket. Also, the financial statements do not show excess foreign tax credits carried forward or back, nor do they show whether the company was subject to the

Alternative Minimum Tax (AMT). Under the laws in effect during the years covered by our data, the AMT often reduced the amount of foreign tax credits the company may claim.[11]

Measuring the Final Foreign Tax Credit Position and Inferring the Anticipated Final Position

We consider the company's final foreign tax credit position for the year to be one of excess credit if the company would not have benefited from being given an extra dollar of foreign tax credits that year, after accounting for its ability to carry excess foreign tax credits over to prior or future years. This final position cannot be measured in all cases, even with a complete time series of data that covers the carry-over years. For example, suppose that in 1997 a company finally would have been able to absorb an extra dollar of foreign tax credits given to it in 1992 (just before they expired), but that this would have reduced the amount of foreign tax credits that it would otherwise have carried back from 1998. Whether or not the company would suffer from the reduction in carry-backs depends on whether or not it would be able to absorb the excess credits it held in 1998 before they expired in 2003, which, in turn, may depend on its carry-backs from 2004, and so forth into the indefinite future.

Despite the problems in measuring the final foreign tax credit position, if the company exports goods from the United States, we can, in some years, infer from its tax return whether it anticipated having excess foreign tax credits for the year after carry-

---

[11] This rule was repealed as part of The American Jobs Creation Act of 2004. For an explanation of how the AMT affected a company's foreign tax credit position, see Lyon and Silverstein (1995).

14

overs. This opportunity arises owing to the interaction of the sales source rules for U.S. export income and the Foreign Sales Corporation (FSC) program.[12] The sales source rules allow a company with excess foreign tax credits to reduce by 50 percent the effective rate of U.S. tax on its export income by deeming up to 50 percent of its export profits as being FSI. Companies with excess credits have an incentive to increase their ratio of FSI to worldwide income in this way, because doing so raises the amount of foreign tax credits they may utilize that year.

The FSC program typically allowed the company to exempt 15 percent of its export income from U.S. tax. If the company used a FSC for the exports, however, then it could use the sales source rules to apply foreign tax credits to only 25 percent of the export income. Used together, the FSC and the sales source rules typically reduced the U.S. tax on a company's U.S. export profits by about 40 percent, whereas if the company applied the sales source rules without using a FSC for the exports, it could reduce the tax on the export profits by 50 percent if it had sufficient excess foreign tax credits.

Stated another way, if the company had excess foreign tax credits that it expected to expire unused, the tax on its export profits would have been 10 percent higher if it had used a FSC for the exports instead of relying exclusively on the sales source rules. On the other hand, if the company anticipated having no unused foreign tax credits, it would have saved 15 percent in taxes on the export profits by using a FSC. Thus, we can infer whether the company anticipated having excess foreign tax credits, after carry-overs,

---

[12] For a more detailed explanation of the FSC program, see U.S. Department of the Treasury (1997). A detailed description of the operation of the sales source rules is provided in U.S. Department of the Treasury (1992). Rousslang (1994) describes the interaction between these programs.

merely by looking to see whether it used a FSC for its exports. In fact, if the company

used a FSC for *any* of its exports, we can infer that it anticipated paying a residual U.S.

tax and therefore its anticipated final position for the year was one of excess limit. For

example, a company with excess foreign tax credits in a given year would have used a

FSC for some of its exports only if, after applying the sales source rules and after

allowing for carry-overs and for the interaction of the FSC and sales source rules, it

anticipated being in final excess limit for the year. Also, a company in excess limit in a

given year would have chosen to forgo using a FSC, and therefore to rely exclusively on

the sales source rules for its export tax saving, only if it had expected to be able to carry

back sufficient excess foreign tax credits from the ensuing two years.[13]

It seems safe to presume that if companies respond to tax incentives at all, they

would have efficiently utilized the two special tax provisions for profits from U.S.

exports, because doing so requires little effort beyond making the appropriate accounting

entries.[14]

---

[13] It is possible that the current foreign tax credit position will be artificially perversely correlated with our measure of the anticipated final position. This is true, because booking exports through a FSC reduces the amount of foreign tax credits that the company can claim by using the sales source rules. For instance, if the company anticipated having excess limit positions in future years, it may have used a FSC for some of its exports in the current year, even if this created more excess foreign tax credits in the year. To account for this effect, we constructed an alternative measure for the company's foreign tax credit position before the increase in FSI created with the sales source rules. This alternative measure is unaltered by the company's FSC usage.

[14] The cost of establishing and operating a FSC was minimal, but use of a FSC required that the title to goods be passed abroad. The exporter could arrange to pass title abroad using nothing more than bookkeeping entries. There seldom were adverse U.S. tax consequences of passing title abroad, and companies could decide whether to book exports through a FSC at the end of the accounting period

The Data

Foreign Income and Foreign Taxes as Reported in Financial Statements

The foreign income reported in the company's financial statement is given by the Compustat variable "Pre-Tax Income – Foreign" (PIFO, or annual data item A273) and the foreign corporate income taxes are given by the Compustat variable "Income Taxes – Foreign" (TXFO, or annual data item A64). To infer the company's foreign tax credit position, we followed the standard procedure that was adopted in previous studies,[15] namely, we compared the rate of foreign taxes (foreign taxes divided by foreign earnings) to the U.S. statutory tax rate on corporate income. The company was deemed to be in excess credit if the rate of foreign taxes was higher than the statutory U.S. rate, and if it was lower the company was deemed to be in excess limit.

Foreign Tax Credits and FSI Reported for the General Basket on the Tax Returns

Because the general basket contains almost all (94 percent) of the FSI for manufacturing companies, we use only information from that basket for our analysis. The manufacturing company's FSI and the associated creditable foreign taxes in the general basket are given on lines 6 and 5, respectively, of Schedule B, Part II, Form 1118. Line 5 gives the total of creditable foreign taxes, including tax credits carried over from prior years. The carry-overs are given separately on line 4. The company has excess foreign tax credits in the current year if the creditable foreign taxes exceeded the latent U.S. tax on the foreign-source income, which is usually the statutory U.S. corporate income tax rate multiplied by the FSI. Otherwise the company would have a residual U.S. tax.

For a company with U.S. exports, the anticipated final credit position for the general basket was inferred by whether the company used a FSC for any of its exports, that is, if it reported exempt foreign trade income on line 10, Schedule B of Form 1120 – FSC (U.S. Income Tax Return of a Foreign Sales Corporation), the form for reporting FSC income. U.S. export income that the company includes in FSI under the sales source rules appears on Part I, Schedule F of Form 1118.

The Results

Constructing the Samples of Companies

We constructed several samples of U.S. companies for 1992 and 1996. To be included in a sample, the company had to be classified as a manufacturer and have positive pre-tax foreign earnings, and it had to pay creditable foreign taxes in the current year at a positive rate below 100 percent of FSI. To be included in Sample 1, the company had to have its financial statement included in the Compustat PC Plus file, and the statement had to identify separately the company's foreign earnings and foreign taxes. To be included in Sample 2, the company had to have its Form 1118 included in Treasury's sample of tax returns. Sample 3, the "matched sample" is the primary sample for our analysis. To be included in Sample 3, the company had to be in Samples 1 and 2, and it had to have used a FSC or the sales source rules for exports.

Comparing the Average Effective Tax Rates Calculated from the Financial Statements
With Those Calculated From the Tax Returns for the General Basket

Table 1 shows the dollar-weighted and the un-weighted averages of the foreign effective tax rates on foreign income as measured from financial statement data and on

---

[15] See the studies cited in footnote 2.

FSI as reported on tax returns for the various samples. For both of our sample years (1992 and 1996), we find no statistically significant difference between the mean of the average effective tax rates as calculated from the financial statements in Sample 1 and that of the matched sample, or between the mean of the average effective tax rates as calculated from the tax returns in Sample 2 and that of the matched sample.

For each sample, the mean of the average effective tax rates calculated from the financial statements is higher than the corresponding mean calculated from the tax returns. This is true for both 1992 and 1996. Also, all of the differences are statistically significant at the 95 percent level using a one-tailed test. The difference in tax rates could have gone either way. For example, the income reported in the financial statement includes foreign losses, whereas these losses are excluded from FSI. Thus, the difference in the treatment of losses tends to cause the average foreign tax rate as calculated from the financial statement to exceed the foreign tax rate as calculated from FSI. On the other hand, FSI excludes non-repatriated foreign earnings, and the US parent is less likely to repatriate low-tax foreign earnings, because they may be exposed to a residual U.S. tax. The foreign earnings reported in financial statements include the non-repatriated earnings. Thus, the difference in the treatment of non-repatriated foreign earnings tends to cause the foreign tax rate as calculated from the FSI to exceed the one calculated from data in the financial statement.

Table 2 compares the foreign earnings and foreign taxes in the financial statements with FSI and foreign taxes eligible for the tax credit as reported in the general basket on the tax returns. After accounting for the differences that could be measured,

19

the foreign earnings reported in financial statements accounted for about 86 percent of the FSI of the manufacturing companies in our sample in 1992 and for about 88 percent in 1996. The differences are smaller between foreign taxes taken from the two sources. Foreign taxes reported in financial statements accounted for 103 percent of the creditable foreign taxes reported on tax returns in 1992 and for 95 percent in 1996.

Table 3 shows the frequency of agreement within Sample 3 (for 1992 and 1996 combined) between a dummy variable indicating the current foreign tax credit positions as inferred from the financial statement (DFS) and a dummy variable indicating the position shown on the tax return, either with (DTW) or without (DTWO) excess foreign tax credits carried over from prior years. Each dummy takes a value of one if the company had (or was deemed to have had) excess foreign tax credits and a value of zero otherwise.

A χ^2 test is used to determine whether the dummy variables are statistically independent of each other. The results of the test are reported in the last column of table 3. The table also shows the simple correlation between each pair of dummies. Since observations for the same company for 1992 and 1996 may not be independent of each other (in which case the χ^2 statistic would be biased), the test is done for two separate pooled samples for 1992 and 1996. The first pooled sample (pooled sample a) omits the observations for a company in 1996 if the company is included in the 1992 sample, and the second pooled sample (pooled sample b) omits observations for a company in 1992 if the company is included in the 1996 sample. The results from the two samples are reported as χ^2 (a) and χ^2 (b). For sample a, DFS and DTW were found to be statistically

20

independent. DFS and DTWO were not statistically different in either sample, but DFS is a very poor predictor for DTWO: The simple correlation between the two variables is extremely low (0.01).[16]

These results do not preclude DFS from being a good, unbiased proxy for the final tax credit position or for the anticipated final position. This is true, because the company's current position often switches from one year to the next, so both DTW and DTWO may be poor predictors for the final position. To demonstrate the fickle nature of the current foreign tax credit positions, we constructed a panel of data for 1992 through 1997, which contains 139 companies. Table 4 shows the frequency with which the companies switched positions (from excess credit to excess limit, or *vice-versa*) over this period when the positions were measured both with and without carry-forwards. Even after carry-forwards, less than a quarter of the firms never switched positions during the period, whereas 38 percent switched positions at least twice. The table also shows that the positions as inferred from the financial statements are also fickle and switched about as often as the positions reported on the tax returns.

Using Discreet Variables to Predict the Anticipated Final Foreign Tax Credit Positions

The dummy variable for the anticipated final position (DRA) takes a value of unity if the company did not use a FSC for any of its exports (the final anticipated position is one of excess credit). Table 5 shows how well DTW, DTWO and DFS do at

---

16 We also compared the averages of the tax rates as calculated from the financial statement for the companies that were in excess credit before and after carry-forwards. Neither average differed significantly from the overall average at the 95 percent level.

predicting DRA.[17] The simple correlation and the χ^2 test for independence is reported in the final column of the table. The correlations are all low, and DTW, DTWO and DFS are all statistically independent of DRA at the five percent level of significance in at least one of the pooled samples.[18]

Using Continuous Variables to Predict the Anticipated Final Foreign Tax Credit Positions

Table 6 provides the results of Probit regressions that use continuous variables to explain the anticipated final position. Separate results are presented for 1992 and 1996. The dependent variable in each regression is DRA. In regression 1, the independent variable is the tax rate on foreign earnings calculated from data in the company's financial statement. In regression 2, the independent variable is the rate of potentially creditable foreign taxes on FSI as reported on the company's tax return. In regression 3, the independent variable is the rate of potentially creditable foreign taxes on FSI, where FSI is measured before application of the sales source rules for U.S. export profits. None of the coefficients of the tax rates was statistically significant at the 90 percent level, indicating that neither the rate of tax on foreign income nor the extent to which the

---

[17] In addition to these three dummy variables, we also compared how well three other candidates would predict DRA. One candidate is a dummy variable that predicts a final position of excess credit only if the company generates excess foreign tax credits in the current year and also carries excess credits forward from a prior year. This candidate is less likely than DTW or DTWO to falsely predict that the final position is excess credit when it is actually excess limit. The two other candidates are DTW and DTWO, measured to account for the effect of the export tax breaks on the company's current foreign tax credit position, as explained in note 13. All of these other candidates were statistically independent from DRA at the 95% level. We also used a panel of data for 1992 to 1997 to try to measure the final position for 1992, but the resultant variable was not significantly correlated with DRA, DFS, DTW or DTWO at the usually accepted levels.

18 The weakest result is for the relation between DTWO and DRA. However, DTWO is also more poorly correlated with DRA than are DTW or DFS.

company is in excess credit or excess limit in a particular year provides much information about its final anticipated position for the year.

Summary and Conclusions

A company's foreign tax credit position often is volatile, switching from excess credit to excess limit from one year to the next. Since the company can carry unused foreign tax credits forward or backward in time, it is hard to predict its final foreign tax credit position for a given year. We have found that the measures commonly used to gauge the company's foreign tax credit position (the position as actually reported on the company's tax return or the position imputed from data in the financial statement) can in many cases provide inconsistent results.

As part of our examination of these two measures of the residual tax used in earlier studies, we devised a variable that logically should reveal the final foreign tax credit position the company anticipates having for the year. The variable was constructed using information gleaned from the company's tax planning behavior, namely how it chose between two tax provisions for U.S. export profits, the sales source rules and the FSC provisions. In many cases, our method does not provide a viable alternative to researchers studying the effects of the residual tax, because it can be applied only for companies that export goods from the United States, and only for the handful of years during which data on operations of the FSCs were collected. Nevertheless, it is a useful tool to assess the other variables as measures of the company's foreign tax credit position.

We found that the two measures used in the earlier studies to gauge the company's foreign tax credit position do not correlate well with our new measure of the revealed anticipated final foreign tax credit position. We believe the lack of correlation among the three measures of credit position draws into question the conclusions of the earlier studies.

References

Adler, Michael. "U.S. Taxation of U.S. Multinational Corporations: A Manual of Computational Techniques and Managerial Decision Rules." In International Finance and Trade, Vol. 2, eds. M. Salant, G. Szego. Cambridge Mass.: Ballinger, 1979.

Altshuler, Rosanne and Harry Grubert. "Balance Sheets, Multinational Financial Policy, and the Cost of Capital at Home and Abroad." NBER Working Paper No. 5810. Cambridge, Mass.: National Bureau of Economic Research, October, 1996.

Altshuler, Rosanne and T. Scott Newlon. "The Effects of U.S. tax Policy on the Income Repatriation of U.S. Multinational Corporations." In Studies in International Taxation, eds. A. Giovannini, R.G. Hubbard and J. Slemrod. Chicago: University of Chicago Press, 1993.

Altshuler, Rosanne, T. Scott Newlon and William C. Randolph. "Do Repatriation Taxes Matter? Evidence from the Tax Returns of U.S. Multinationals." In M. Feldstein, J.R. Hines and R.G. Hubbard, eds. The Effects of Taxation on Multinational Corporations. Chicago: National Bureau of Economic Research, 1995.

Collins, Julie, Deen Kemsley and Mark Lang. "Cross-Jurisdictional Income Shifting and Earnings Valuation." Journal of Accounting Research Vol. 36 (Autumn 1998): 209-230.

Dworin, Lowell. "On Estimating Corporate Tax Liabilities From Financial Statements." Tax Notes (December 2, 1985): 965-971.

Froot, Kenneth A. and James R. Hines. "Interest Allocation Rules, Financing Patterns, and the Operations of Multinationals." In M Feldstein, J.R. Hines and R.G. Hubbard, eds. The Effects of Taxation on Multinational Corporations, Chicago: National Bureau of Economic Research, 1995.

Grubert, Harry. "Taxes and the Division of Foreign Operating Income Among Royalties, Interest, Dividends and Retained Earnings." Journal of Public Economics, Vol 68 (May 1998): 269-290.

Hartman, David. "Tax Policy and Foreign Direct Investment." Journal of Public Economics (February 1985): 107-121.

Hines, James R. "Dividends and Profits: Some Unsubtle Foreign Influences." Journal of Finance Vol. 51 (June 1996): 661-689.

Hines, James R., Jr. and R. Glenn Hubbard. "Coming Home to America: Dividend Repatriations by U.S. Multinationals." In Taxation in the Global Economy, ed. A. Razin and J. Slemrod. Chicago: University of Chicago Press, 1990.

Internal Revenue Service, "Corporate Foreign Tax Credit, 1992: An industry and Geographic Focus," Statistics of Income Bulletin, Winter 1995-1996, Washington D.C., 1996.

Kemsley, Deen. "The Effect of Taxes on Production Location." Journal of Accounting Research Vol. 36 (Autumn 1998): 321-342.

Lyon, Andrew B. and Gerald Silverstein. "The Alternative Minimum Tax and the Behavior of Multinational Corporations." In M. Feldstein, J.R. Hines and R.G. Hubbard, eds. The Effects of Taxation on Multinational Corporations. Chicago: National Bureau of Economic Research, 1995.

Mutti, John. "Tax Incentives and the Repatriation Decisions of U.S. Multinational Corporations." National Tax Journal Vol. 34 (June 1981): 241-248.

Rousslang, Donald J. "The Sales Source Rules for U.S. Exports: How Much Do They Cost?" Tax Notes International (February 21, 1994): 527-535, and Tax Notes (February 21, 1994): 1047-1054.

The Mc-Graw Hill Companies. Data Guide, Compustat (North America), 1998.

U.S. Department of the Treasury. The Operation and Effect of the Foreign Sales Corporation Legislation. Washington, D.C.: U.S. Department of the Treasury, November 1997.

U.S. Department of the Treasury. Report on the Sales Source Rules. Washington, D.C.: U.S. Department of the Treasury, 1992.

Table 1: Average Effective Tax Rates for Various Samples of U.S. Manufacturers

Samples 1 and 2
U.S. manufacturers that had positive FSI
and paid foreign tax on the FSI at a positive rate less than 100 percent

	Tax rate calculated from financial statement data (from sample 1)		Rate of creditable foreign taxes on FSI (from sample 2)	
	1992	1996	1992	1996
Number of companies	261	449	453	624
Assets (in $billions)	1,016	1,989	1,669	2,824
Average tax rate:				
Dollar-weighted	0.353	0.334	0.302	0.297
	(0.169)	(0.166)	(0.175)	(0.181)
Un-weighted	0.366	0.339	0.232	0.238
	(0.168)	(0.166)	(0.139)	(0.161)
Median tax rate	0.353	0.327	0.243	0.243

Sample 3
U.S. manufacturers that had positive FSI,
that paid foreign tax on the FSI at a positive rate less than 100 percent,
that used the sales source rules or a FSC for their exports,
and for which tax return and financial statement data are available

	Tax rate calculated from financial statement data		Rate of creditable foreign taxes on FSI	
	1992	1996	1992	1996
Number of companies	168	299	168	299
Assets (in $billions)	874	1,753	874	1,753
Average tax rate:				
Dollar-weighted	0.349	0.330	0.285	0.289
	(0.166)	(0.154)	(0.135)	(0.164)
Un-weighted	0.383	0.335	0.264	0.255
	(0.162)	(0.154)	(0.129)	(0.155)
Median tax rate	0.359	0.330	0.283	0.273

Note: The figures in parentheses are standard deviations.

Table 2: Reconciling Income and Taxes as Reported on Tax Returns and in Financial Statements for the Companies in Sample 3

(In millions of dollars)

Income Reconciliation:	1992	1996
General basket FSI..	19,147	55,423
minus:		
Distributions from prior years' E&P....................................	5,629	10,839
Current year losses of CFCs..	2,814	5,122
Interest and royalties from related parties...........................	3,929	15,458
Net income included in FSI under the sales source rules......	3,544	10,477
plus:		
Domestic expenses charged against FSI...............................	8,172	23,921
Non-repatriated E&P[†]..16,053		43,589
FSI in other baskets, except the FSC basket		
and the passive income basket,		
less creditable foreign income taxes in the		
section 902 baskets...	772	2,509
Total:...	28,228	83,546
Foreign income as reported in		
financial statements..	24,393	73,897
Unreconciled difference in foreign income............................	3,835	9,649

Tax Reconciliation:		
Creditable taxes in the general basket	5,417	15,769
plus		
Creditable taxes in other baskets,		
except the 902 basket..	267	1,172
Foreign taxes on non-repatriated E&P		
of majority-owned foreign subsidiaries[†]..................................	4,334	11,769
minus:		
Creditable taxes attributable to distributions		
from prior years' E&P	1,730	3,040
Total:	8,288	25,670
Foreign taxes as reported in		
financial statements	8,502	24,360
Unreconciled difference in foreign taxes...................................	-214	1,310

[†] Estimated using a tax calculator developed by the Office of Tax Analysis, U.S. Department of Treasury.

[††] Total FSI of the manufacturing companies in all baskets was 20,667 in 1992 and 60,060 in 1996. The total of their foreign taxes in all baskets was 5,684 in 1992 and 16,941 in 1996.

Table 3: The Frequency of Agreement Between the Foreign Tax Credit Position as Reported on Tax Returns and as Inferred from Financial Statements

Pooled observations from sample 6 for 1992 and 1996

DFS	DTW			
	Excess Credit	Excess Limit	Total	$r=0.11$
Excess Credit	103	124	227	$\chi^2(a)=9.70*$
Excess Limit	84	156	240	$\chi^2(b)=0.76$
Total	187	280	467	
DFS	DTWO			
	Excess Credit	Excess Limit	Total	$r=0.01$
Excess Credit	56	171	227	$\chi^2(a)=2.34$
Excess Limit	57	183	240	$\chi^2(b)=0.70$
Total	113	354	467	

Note: DTW is the position reported on the tax return after carry-forwards, DFS is the position inferred from the financial statement, and DTWO is the position reported on the tax return before carry-forwards. An asterisk (*) indicates that the χ^2 is significant at the 95% level or better.

Table 4: The Frequency with which Companies Switch Foreign Tax Credit Positions:
1992 to 1997

Foreign tax credit position after carry-forwards

Number of switches	Number of companies	Percent of total	Cum. Percent
0	33	23.7	23.7
1	53	38.1	61.8
2	30	21.6	83.4
3	16	11.5	94.9
4	6	4.3	99.2
5	1	0.8	100.0
Total:	139	100.0	

Foreign tax credit positions before carry-forwards

Number of switches	Number of companies	Percent of total	Cum. Percent
0	27	19.4	19.4
1	42	30.2	49.6
2	40	28.8	78.4
3	20	14.4	92.8
4	6	4.3	97.1
5	4	2.9	100.0
Total:	139	100.0	

Foreign tax credit positions based on COMPUSTAT data

Number of switches	Number of companies	Percent of total	Cum. Percent
0	39	26.5	26.5
1	34	23.1	49.6
2	47	32.0	81.6
3	21	14.3	95.9
4	5	3.4	99.3
5	1	0.7	100.0
Total:	147	100.0	

Table 5: Frequency of an Agreement between the Anticipated Final Foreign Tax Credit Position as Inferred from the Use of Export Tax Breaks and Various other Candidates that Might be Used to Infer the Anticipated Final Position

Non-overlapping Pooled observations for 1992 and 1996

	DRA			
DTW	Excess Credit	Excess Limit	Total	$r=0.12$
Excess Credit	60	127	187	$\chi^2(a)=7.26^*$
Excess Limit	59	221	280	$\chi^2(b)=6.82^*$
Total	119	348	467	
	DRA			
DTWO	Excess Credit	Excess Limit	Total	$r=0.09$
Excess Credit	37	76	113	$\chi^2(a)=5.24^*$
Excess Limit	82	272	354	$\chi^2(b)=3.13$
Total	119	348	467	
	DRA			
DFS	Excess Credit	Excess Limit	Total	$r=0.11$
Excess Credit	69	158	227	$\chi^2(a)=7.75^*$
Excess Limit	50	190	240	$\chi^2(b)=5.82^*$
Total	119	348	467	

Note: Please see the note to table 3. DRA is a dummy variable representing the anticipated final tax credit position as inferred from the company's use of the sales source rules and the FSC for its exports.

Table 6: Continuous Variable Candidates for Determining the Anticipated Final Position

Observations are for exporting manufacturing companies
Probit regressions, Dependent variable: DRA

Year	1992	1996
Independent variable	Coefficient (and χ^2)	
Regression 1:	n = 168	n = 299
Constant	0.26 (1.33)	0.79 (23.92)*
Rate of creditable foreign taxes on FSI (from tax returns)	0.11 (0.02)	0.50 (0.81)
Regression 2:	n = 168	n = 299
Constant	0.36 (1.96)	1.21 (33.02)*
Rate of tax on foreign earnings (from financial statements)	-0.18 (0.09)	-0.86 (2.44)
Regression 3:	n = 166	n = 298
Constant	0.31 (9.54)*	0.91 (96.89)*
Rate of creditable foreign taxes on FSI before application of the sales source rules (from tax returns)	-0.04 (1.06)	0.12 (0.02)

Note: An asterisk (*) indicates that the χ^2 is significant at the 95 percent level or better.

www.ingramcontent.com/pod-product-compliance
Lightning Source LLC
Chambersburg PA
CBHW052026280526
45793CB00005B/1136